THE BONES OF CREATION

First published in 2008 by
The Dedalus Press
13 Moyclare Road
Baldoyle
Dublin 13
Ireland

www.dedaluspress.com

ISBN 978 1 904556 92 3 (bound)
ISBN 978 1 904556 91 6 (paper)

Dedalus Press titles are represented in North America
by Syracuse University Press, Inc., 621 Skytop Road,
Suite 110, Syracuse, New York 13244, and in the UK by
Central Books, 99 Wallis Road, London E9 5LN

Typesetting and design: Pat Boran
Cover image © Amanda Rohde

The Dedalus Press receives financial assistance from
An Chomhairle Ealaíon / The Arts Council, Ireland

THE BONES OF CREATION

Patrick Deeley

DEDALUS PRESS
DUBLIN, IRELAND

ACKNOWLEDGEMENTS

Acknowledgements are due to the editors of the following in which a number of these poems, or versions of them, originally appeared:

Irish Pages, The Stinging Fly, Poetry Ireland Review, Our Shared Japan (Dedalus Press), *Cyphers, Sud-Est Cultural* (Moldova), *The French Literary Review, Envoi, The Backyards of Heaven* (WIT), *Crannóg, Southword, Wingspan: A Dedalus Sampler, Brass On Bronze* (Errigal Writers Anthology), *Something Beginning With P* (O'Brien Press) and *The SHop*.

In Memory of Pat Whelan,
Co-Founder of the Irish Fostercare Association

Contents

THE BONES OF CREATION

If I am made to feel small under the stars,
and my looking beyond the moon
into black dungeons of space
is futile, again I must turn to grounded things,

crawl of woodlouse and beetle, boulder
slowly going to pieces, off-shoot
of crack and crevice where the mite works,
and the bacterium. And if I no more

have eyes for earth than for the sky's vastness,
still the grey shade of hope attends
my notion of a next-to-no-size creature
supporting a creature a million times smaller—

on a whisker, say, that sprouts
in the tunnel of its ear, or on the prayer
it offers up, whether breathing or not breathing,
from the flowing bones of creation.

One of a Kind

Then this tough vegetative tangle,
couchant under the weight
of altitude, is stumbled on
in a valley in the Andes—by a man
who suspects that what

he's found is one of a kind,
and plucks a sample. Laboratory
analysis reveals a fossil tree
propagating itself, each
stubborn step, each fix and twist

in the colonising sprawl
an encapsulation of centuries.
If not quite immortal, surely
a Methuselah lives at large, a wonder
of the wilderness. Maybe

yet to find itself, after a makeover,
at home in gardens where still
the dream of a waterfall or wood,
a plant or animal surviving
undiscovered, comes to replenish

an outback in our minds,
to wend us towards a secret held
beyond the mountains,
plumbed oceans, found and fumbled
world caught in our map's net.

Dandelions

The longest yields a three-foot root;
the shortest squeaks a snaggy tail. Sod
and spade, where would I be going?

Not out with the diners tonight.
The bouquet of restaurant will have to do,
breeze-borne from four doors down.

And this lawn, lit with dandelions.
Their stalks break bitter milk on my skin;
they give nothing unless they give

everything—the withheld scrap
comes up in clusters. And I, levering them
through mats of grass with meticulous

gentleness, lull myself into believing
I loved them in an earlier time.
There seemed to be room then, abundance

of wildflower places, but these
were weeds still—they brought me
to my knees, I cursed tillage, the big darkness

fell, the world wheeled by, suiting itself
until I forgot and was forgotten,
and grew alone, and knew this was natural.

On Ice

Five or six of us, deciding school is shut,
leave the slidey pavement
and go skating half a mile out
to where a biplane has landed
on the frozen lake, and shout up close
at such a flimsy thing,

rigged with raggy canvas
and bits of rope, and shake it
in its skeletal standing, and marvel
that it might be made to ride the air, to glide
and dive. Which it does
only in our mouthed sound-effects.

Until the shore begins to seem
very far, the whitened hills unfamiliar,
the boat-house a blur we lean
towards, pushing through
our billowing breaths. "Just don't let
the ice break," someone shouts,

hurrying us who've heard the legend
of how the old, first and best town
exists still, deep under the lake.
A place that is palatial, lit by green and blue,
where those too good for this world
are taken. And here now

we sense the child of seven summers,
so unaltered, so unafraid,
ascending past his slick
shimmering rooftops, gazing unblinking up
at our frantic, flurrying feet,
our red cries—and wistful, too.

Keaveney's Well

Didn't ask who Keaveney was,
just took everything off—shoes, clothes,
sunhat—just took yourself
away from sweat and haymaking,
slid between low walls. It
might have been a stone coffin,
one of those ancient cists,
possessions arrayed about you
except that here the cold
submergence burned—senses said
you hadn't lived before this
steeping of your bones. Clay
and marl juices seeped;
cress, pond lily tickled; the one-minded
school of minnow turned.
Land was aspiring to be water;
water wanted to be land.
A trembling happened, a bubble
spun glistening, then the great
taboo tail of the subterranean river rose;
you dreamed the evening
women come to dunk their pails.

Callows-Water Barrel

The goldfish turns silver, then black, enlarges
with the passing years to make a legend.
The tadpole destined to stay forever limbless
extends until the length of your hand.
The minnow outgrows its name. Child,
you seek for such things as can't be proved
by trawling a butterfly net. Your
imagination runs deeper, and deeper yet.
Through the murky bottom of a Callows-water
barrel, past spits of mud and grit,
under the secret river shilly-shallying
between Mullagh Beg and Keaveney's Well.
Until you become the world's fool hereabouts—
far gone by nature into the mire, with
dwelling loneliness your dreamed-up behemoth.

Territory

Ben Bán, even Poppyhill, will be tall enough
to feature in the finished picture. As will
everything. Climb prepared to remain
until cloud and hazes clear. Detail the sweep
from Scalp to Inis Mór, lines that river,
tree lines, dry-stone walls, coasts that seem
hardly other than notional. Haul up
the theodolite of steep and undulant images.
With nightfall, let the limelight be on fox
or badger answering to your stillness.
What matter if all was better said and done
before? Now you are leased the wonder
of fitting grey-eyed Lough Rea in, of gritting
beside it the statue to Stoney Brennan,
hanged for stealing a turnip. Leased the city
of teeming tribes, technology's wavering
landscape, lane and fieldname slipped, ring-fort
turned roundabout. Leased the puzzle
of where Shannon's Callows begin and end,
whose the dent on a cannonball found at
Aughrim, what the mother word for Kilrickle.

Muslin

The island woman came ashore on a bigger island,
settled away from the sea. Her Gaelic dried
in her throat for want of answering. Her lore
was shrugged off by the new people. She held to
her shawl. And when the local children
bundled in, she sent them to the shops on small
errands. Unwinding—it always seemed
to take an age, and it always stilled them—her pennies
from a measure of muslin she could trail
to a ship the sea had washed up, sixty years before.

The Marl Excavations

The dankest imaginable smell comes up
when you pull a flaggard, shank
and root, out of the soft spongy moot
where the Callows river meanders
to a standstill. Black earth smell,
but not that of the bog, which is civil
by comparison. No, you inhale
now a great conglomeration—rust
ooze, insect oil, fetid vegetation,
drowned horse, sheep, heifer, diluted
droppings of the long-gone crake,
plover, Greenland goose and gander.
Yet you must lean down further in,
squeeze pottage of fibrous soil
between your fingers, hold it close
to your nostrils. Because it alerts you
to the hare's-form squat of childhood,
the marl excavations: white, with
small tell-tale shells remembering a lake
where the Callows found its first
foothold—and where your heart's
pangs are shallow waves, breaking still.

The Bee-Sting

The pulsing of the honeybee's abdomen
as she crawled along my arm,
the scraping, snaggy feel of her limbs—
I couldn't help but shiver. This

was a wrong move. The abdomen
dipped, the sting struck home. I burned
and burned. And then, because
there seemed no worse thing to expect,

I watched while she dragged about
in a circle before finally breaking
away to die. But the venom sac,
the barbed, embedded thorn, twitched

of their own accord—pumping,
emptying. And I daydreamed these
were the merest scraps of a giant dragon
that wouldn't and couldn't die,

raising always out of brokenness
a mending or an attempted mending.
For such was nature to me, such
was nature's dragon will, all my tremor

matched by the sigh of a wise woman
who came possessed of her own
cure, to sit me on a flagstone and say:
"Child, the sting that doesn't kill

keeps you supple." And I found
the shorn antenna dancing still. The twig
successfully sown. The beheaded
earthworm regenerating on the double.

Night

I looked up the kitchen chimney.
An echo chamber floating
amid soot tempted me to shout,
but then my father's snores

came trembling down the stairs.
Night was otherwise hushed
huge, full of potency that forbade.
Old-men jackdaws roosted.

The old-jackdaw men had tapped
their pipes empty, departed
with a spit. Their stories fingered
my spine, so many chill tingles.

I saw one framed star, faint and far
from meaning in the black
heavens as my own constrained life
amid the dying ashes. What

had the stories intended? Something
I might live to discover—
that the fort field, the Callows tree,
everywhere I had made free,

was haunted. That water and wind
and light played on the world
in ways I'd be foolish to upset. That
for all this, life was open-ended.

Wellspring

One more story coming out of the earth
sees this slimed creature hauled
onto a flagstone, sludge in his boots
and hair. There's a stone-bruise
at his navel and he smells, as the rope
untied from his waist, of gravel.

All day he has hacked the grime out,
sent it by the bucket-load up
through the whirling, dripping air,
who now is the last one looking
down. Below, the gouged-out chamber
sits, its floor leaking bubbles

in the darkness, and gurgles, and chill
rivulets cleanly trickling. Though
he doesn't say so yet, this well
will draw a village to haul its water
home. It will see out drought
and deluge. It will be the measure

against which he sets city fountain
and burst main. Stooping under pretext
of tying his bootlace, he will study
the dimples made by raindrops
on a pavement puddle, he will
address the scars of a passing breeze,

and feel himself begin to compose—
the weathered day, the settlement
of mud, the well envisioned, swollen
to its brim. His grey reflection
will be cast in. He will straighten as if
still wearing these stone clothes.

Capstone

This garden wall is cherished by more
than me alone. The roses and
the apple branches rising up
out of its grimy foot, stand sheltered.
And the sun, taking all day
to come round the houses, lingers

in every crevice, every mossy spot.
At evening, a game of bluff
is played between two magpies
and a feral cat. And when darkness
falls, woodlice climb to graze
damp pastures of peeling whitewash.

The wall's crumbling, pocked
and blotched. Here, my gritted elbows
sit. Here a crown of ivy was
blown off. And here, dream-garden
possibilities present themselves—
foliated, trained and trellised

along fancy brickwork. Still I keep
to a bargain struck with the rain
and the powdering frosts—
a wall stands, there is fervour even in
a forgetful head, something held
sacred under this slipping capstone.

On the Stone Machine

She is shooting me from her separate
cubicle, shooting me through
and through as if directly
under my left kidney. Forty minutes
strapped up here, the cold gel
applied, and her face visible
at the cubicle window, her hands
busy aiming. Who would think
as I take in the *thrip, thrip, thrip*—
two thousand magic bullets
before I'm done—that a video game
could transmogrify so wittily
to a medical procedure? The stone
in my shoe I would pluck out
readily as a child, but the shoe
itself, too tight, all the pairs of shoes
always a crush confounding me
with misshapen toes. Cat pinched
my squeak? Not cat, more
the way a customary pain becomes
second nature, only give it time.
And the day's slow ritual of socks
peeled off, socks hand-wrung,
turns vivid now as childhood
sunsets in my head, as water sloshed
about in old enamel basins
pooling red. Elastic slaps, the stone
machine's pins and needles
quicken. I learn the sympathy
a stoneless kidney holds for a kidney
with a stone. Until all is a song,

the body's shakes and stutters
belonging to everyone and no-one,
even down to particularities
of pissing blood later on. Until all
is pain—which I am to signal, should
it prove unbearable, by raising
my hand for the lady of the console.

The Caileach

On the shore at Beara, the caileach
finally comes a cropper,
dashes into and fuses with a stone.

Or so the myth tells. It's implied
that she started out beautiful,
desirable, obedient, good—the words

are interchangeable. In the course
of the myth she develops
a taste for sorcery, dissension,

herbs and potions injurious to what
the pharmacists of the day
might sell. Domestic duties

fly out the door; she grows slovenly
and wild. Warts accrue about
her nose; she sports the gossip's

big chin. A saint wanders
into the picture, or maybe a bishop.
She takes a shine to his

magic stick made of Bog of Allen oak.
He chases her to the shore
at Beara, the summary petrifaction.

If the myth's laughable now,
with the caileach seeming to flourish
as she pleases, there is still

a woman can tell how hard and for
how long she herself—in
the manner of her mother before her

and her mother's mother—has
had to bang her head against the stone,
to wear it down, make it open.

The Sill

Shortly before he was broken, I caught
the shake in his hand as he reached
for the stone slab that served
as a church window sill. I was a stranger

home for the weekend, famous, it
seemed, now that I had a book of poems
to my name. Or so said my credulous
neighbours, who would as soon

leave poems unread. But who was
the more misled—they or I, or this faltering
priest who yet appeared to have faith
in the words he wanted from me

for the cold, blue-tinted stone
that someone, centuries past, had saved
following an altar's desecration?
My would-be inspirer's hand tapped

and traced as if deciphering a Latin text,
then trembled from the sill, unable
to contain the enthusiasm of his telling.
And I had inkling of the stroke

that would sweep from him the wherewithal
to kneel or genuflect. I fit words
together still, pit them against the dead
weight of oblivion. And on a visit

back, re-echo the clumsy, mumbled, get-out
clause I gave him in place of a poem.
And lean on this stone that has so long
stood for more than his or my consolation.

A Burrishoole Gate

All the days we pass through, it swings
from where its two sections
of rickety timber are tied with twine
at the centre, swings in the wind

that blusters full against our faces.
We call it 'wind gate'. It makes no sense
because it marks no point
of exit or entry, and adjoins no fence

other than a ditch we'd as surely cross
with half the hindrance. Below
and above and about it, nature happens
too hugely for any containment.

The run of laughing rivulets, the shifting
mist in cahoots with the bare
heads of the hills, the rainbow spanning
a lake—these powers beyond

the powers of reckon and render
that would have us quarry a mountain
down, or bulldoze a wilderness
to accommodate a rubbish dump, seem now

the subtle setting of the world
to rights: we watch them come and go,
fade and flourish, free in the open
country round a Burrishoole wind gate.

Fossils

If our forebears lifting these stones,
carrying them clear of pasture
and plough, clamping them up
to make the mearings, ever set eyes
on scallop or whelk, fossilised

here where land is high and dry
and far from seashore, they must have
passed no remarks, at least
none loud enough to last us as lore.
Instead, we register our children's

shouts; they hurry their haul
of select stones down, shaping
with hammer and chisel as if to pave
the ocean's return. Only fantail
or whorl-effect distinguishes

creatures they unfetter, creatures
petrified in mud long before the earth
was peopled. Tip-tap, wallop—
our words about respect for fences
are lost in face of solid wonder.

A fossil nugget flies free. They break
into a run, fumble to retrieve it.
Their hands semaphore; vaguely
we discern them, shimmering through
heat-haze at the end of our vision.

Autumnal Tree at the Garden's Foot

Send me six colours now,
your top leaves golden,
your lowermost green,
with silver wind-turned bellies,
grey bole, red berries,
and a name: white beam.

Birdsong

Perspectives through sound: a blackbird's
oath, sworn from a chimney-stack;
the mellifluous coos of woodpigeons
conjuring sunbeams amid high ivy clusters;
a robin's pipe, happening to approve
of cotoneaster berries. But if the tremulous,
piercing notes of the thrush are
expansions of space and time, rolling me
wide and far, I still hear the magpie's
screeched assertion from a wall overlooking
the covered-in quarry, that all was
winter yesterday, was stone the day before.

Frogs

No barrel of laughs, hoisting
a broken-backed bridge
out of the stream
with grapnel and crowbar,
with bare hands.

All's discolouring sludge,
marl you must plunge
down into. Until a sudden
jumble of frogs.
They've sat through winter,

cold customers
still blazoned with harvest's
golden overcoat,
still fat. Dandle them
on your shovel, pass them up

to exterior grass.
Everything lies in wait,
mower and drought,
beak of bird, the fox's snout;
everything's to suffer

yet, even the dead season
springing a frosty tail.
These must leap far, carry far
the world they contain
entire. Softly cast them off.

Cave Life

If limestone asserts the sea
once stood taller than this inland hill,
limestone only begins to shape
the twisting tale. There is never

simply nothing further—we go
through squeezes, down.
Sunless for a million years, creatures
can have no use of colour.

Slowly the long dark quenches
their eyes, skin finds ways
to redefine itself and them. Bat radar
is turned on, the snake's

knack of tracking heat. Antennae
extend, frail yet fitted to tap
the convolutions of crevice
and crystal. Change hazards everything,

and we are not immune. Heads
swelling in our acceleration
of knowledge and pride render us
the more prone to topple.

But that here we stop, humbled under
wonder-wheels of calcite fruits
and flowers, of beast and angel shapes
with all the time in the world

at their disposal; here we dream
our first emergence from the rock, our
bald skulls smooth stalagmites
splashed by exploding water drops.

Gargoyle

It grips high up next the roof of an old
cathedral, and if you glance from
a certain spot—downhill across the street—
you see grass growing out of its skull,
a garland of grass and moss. And one

tiny clot of red poppy, waving above
the grey monstrosity. You catch
its fissured grin, mounded shoulders,
dragonesque of webs and scales, and stop
dead in your tracks. Then you tell

yourself it's petrified, and could
never come down. You recall, or try to,
the centuries through which it's clung,
designed to scare away the demons
people believed in. Except now that you've

moved closer, it doesn't cling, it wheels
about frightful of face and ever
so light on its reptilian feet. Which makes
you think *it* is the demon! But what
comes spluttering from its throat—

blood or screams or an ancient garbled song—
is your imagination. So look again.
Those wrinkles and worry lines, those
cracked eyes trickling wetness, will plead
there's a weathered, inanimate thing

yet tries to live, gathering particles of dust
as they rise, gathering even traffic-smoke
and flakes of shed skin, nourishing
wind-blown spores and seeds, that it
might speak to you one day only in flowers.

Tabernacle

No sightseer totes his fickle
worship here, no saboteur
his blaspheming bomb or gun.
A cordon of authorised
deadly force states itself.

Rattlesnake and tumbleweed,
though native to this place,
are rendered alien now in face
of the scientific tabernacle.
I dream of Mars and Orion,

bellicose terms billeted
skyward, of Lucifer flung
in a founding dream of heaven
from pinnacle to chasm.
And there's no end to warfare

or to thought. Second
by second billions of calculations
happen inside a synthetic
yolk sac cooled, as the heart
under surgery is, by blood

substitute. Will we fall
to the brute 'ultimate rationale',
circuits commandeering
a shield in outer space, 'brilliant
eyes' scanning the way God

in our childhood was said
to have done, 'space pebbles'
primed to defend us—or to attack?
Look up at our iniquities,
O tumbleweed, O rattlesnake.

Species

I might find them subsisting still
in soggy Callows, on the sides
of ditches, in old graveyards—those
herbs, wildflowers, grasses
that put the first spring in my step;
I might pluck their names from
an almanac: vetch, bird's-foot
trefoil, orchid, summer snowflake...
Then to inhale the smells, be
dizzied again, bear with grace what
rash or hay fever was on offer.
I might even bring myself to touch
the last, exquisitely dappled
boggle-eyed caterpillar, set a ripple
running through it, shout my father
back from the brink of ecological
disaster, lead him by his grainy
fertilizer hand to stoop with me there,
over wonders of cuckoo spit,
spider and cowslip, on a headland.

Piecework

Mushrooms could become their own lamps,
flickering on and off, though I never
discovered whether this was a mechanism

of spore-dispersal or of self-defence—
I simply picked them, threaded a traithnín
through the pedestal of each in turn,

and carried my bundle home. Sheep pasture,
damp autumn, mushrooms would
spring up overnight. Bog-English was

the only language spoken. We'd be
turnip-snaggers all our lives, the master said.
He had us measured for the sleán

and shovel.
                    Boys and girls of my childhood,
I try to map your exile now, I strain
my ear to catch your altered accents. And

perhaps you in your idle moments
return to a misty morning picking mushrooms
in our Callows, a free-range life before

world found altogether new meanings. Or
maybe you'd as soon forget this land
forced to sump and mulch, its wet meadows

drained, its people shifting out from
back field to main road, its menial undercoat
hidden, the long tunnels where the Polish

and Latvian women move, pale-skinned
in semi-darkness, pushing through piecework
with their baskets of button mushrooms.

Appearances

The etching of an urn adorns
your door, flowers
toppling out, marigolds and ferns.
You know the silverwork
is fake, eaten through with rust
where the slender neck
into the rounded shoulder
ought to be flowing.
It's said you've lost your head—
the caved-in ceiling, the gas-ring
a sputtering blue corona
always on, upstairs the thunder
of the cistern tethered
to an ancient chain. You don't
feel misled; the colour
of rust deepens, re-gathering
a fox you let scatter
in childhood, the cistern
sets streamlets flooding far Callows,
your worlds to the world
at large insists life's
a frittering minute, beauty
the breaking nature of everything.

After the Mining at Tynagh

When I recall the wild meadow
silver and zinc won't re-grow,

a river flows un-circumvented
through me here, where cyanide

doesn't wash, any more
than mining lease or iron ore.

So that out of the time spent
on a thought, I reinvent

daisy, buttercup, timothy, rye,
clover and cowslip behind my eye,

let walls wed snails, bushes
in turn lead to mated thrushes.

Then earth mouth, mile-deep
mine shaft, dead landscape

scalped and slagged, rusted air-
compressor caved under

a concrete hangar, multi-flanged
seized-up generator, deranged

stone crusher, all grow again
innocent of the doings of men.

And in the derelict hall
where some of us, born gullible,

once credited 'a new strain
of grass, re-pasturing the mine',

centipedes and millipedes weave
their own versions of love

under a soggy carpet, toadstools
break through cracks in tiles,

mice make haphazard shredders
of yellowed company ledgers.

Say no ground's ever fully dead,
step a mound of musty weed,

find a mushroom pushing through
the pickled plumage of a crow.

Castigate my hurt, lack of patience
with the dirt, cite endurance

of little things that are humbling
inklings of a new beginning.

Call it all a necessary process—
I'm dreaming still nature in place,

though ages may come and go
and my dream not make a meadow.

The Last Seanchai

His laugh comes from below the belly,
below the groin, and his laugh
shakes him all the way up. He slaps
his thighs to help the laugh
along, he tickles his sides. His laugh's

a familiar animal in our rambling house,
or rather several animals which
he keeps contained while the story
opens across familiar fields,
Carrowshanbally to Eskerboy.

Between the lighting of his pipe
and the first spit in the fire, events take
a delicious or a drastic turn.
These spellbound faces, our parents
young again, these lame old men

redrawn to vigour, these holy women
gone funny in serious places—
what are we to make of them?
Nothing, now his story's at an end,
and we listen past the punch line

for a hoarse lock turning
in his throat, a rusty wheeze as of
gates opening, before the pent-up beasts
of merriment burst forth, neigh
and bray, squeal and howl, and all

our lesser beasts of laughter
lift, gambol among them—this must be
the resuscitation of winter earth,
this the perpetual moonshine
where play the dead, this the hearth-song

we will scarcely recognise as
having belonged to us, after he is made
to exit blinking from the sight
of the TV in the corner, with his
'God save all here' stopped on his tongue.

Taking Fire

The lilac come to flower on a chimney's shoulder
would make for a hero but that the chimney
is my own. I've no thought but to climb
and tear the upstart from red-brick as I might ivy
or moss or a jackdaw's nest. The poem
climbs ahead of me, condemning the intent,
offering a dirge to pilfered nature, to rugged hills
whirling windmills, to rivers dammed. I dream
I can see for a hundred miles, all the way
to the road-works at Cappataggle. There, a stoat
leads six young across the ruptured land.
Her white, sidewise snarl is encouragement enough
to turn me round. So I sway with the lilac,
taking fire equably from the chimney and the sky.

The City's at Home

Night skies of my childhood, the city's
at home where I could count on your stars.
Will-o'-the-wisp's a high-watt lantern—
did I only dream the quaking *wet meadow*?

"Stories will travel on top of sticks,"
my great grand-uncle got up to prophesy.
His fireside hob, where I could hear
crickets piping, has yielded to the hub,

the digital handshake. What surprise, then,
a cow path booming into motorway,
a bog sliding on its belly down from
Derrybrien, the wide world come to pass?

Simulation

The red squirrels take off
away from you across the grass,
towards the trees, whose
trunks they will climb—always
in close, roundhouse runs.

The ducks stop grazing
and scatter at your approach,
becoming airborne, splashing
down where the pond's
widest. But if you cause

disturbances, you settle
at the same time everything back
in what you consider its
natural element. And receive
the bonus of close-ups:

a furry face, a frittered acorn,
a loose feather gone
dithering airily onto another
level. There, the swan
sails in apparent serenity

past her inelegant offspring,
to hiss in your face, to raise
a bone-breaker wing. It's
a game, of course, and if the red
squirrels are pushed out

by your introduction of
the greys, if the mallards fail
to spot poisons you've set
for rats, if the swans asphyxiate
on synthetics or bottle-tops,

you can revert to the beginning.
So the red squirrels take
off away from you across
the grass—towards the trees,
whose trunks they will climb.

To the Wintering Virginia Creeper

You appear—tall tale holding to pebble-dash—
a subterranean giant whose arm and claw
draws off the central heat, grappling
even with the slates of the house. Your reach
seems all of nature, though crocus
and snowdrop peep, and rust-throated tulip
bells in silence a promise of brightness
from its nook. You're rattled by the wind,
old brittle-sticks, whose roots I can no nearer
track to source—too many rock-twists
about a wall—than my own forked
and fumbling intellect. Which now, to satisfy
a famished aesthete, would see you greened
again, wreathing round each window sill, your
small stealth on shrewd feet sprouting,
your settling passion a ribbon of roseate
leaflets, borne over the new season's threshold.

Mistletoe

A bird scrapes its beak on a branch
of oak, or dribbles its droppings there.
Unwittingly a seed is set. This

requires only sap's nurture. It plugs itself
into tree-power. The arrangement's
sealed with a disc. Out of which

mistletoe comes—evergreen, antlered.
Now we're swayed to the mood
of the disgruntled primitive, glancing

about for evidence of a bud.
Now his joy is ours as we discern
the leafy wonder surviving still

in a winter-bare wood. Should we call it
'all healer', or 'gift from the sky god'?
Or take such ceremonial pains as

the oak-man took to counter grief,
raise a blade and nick the elevated parasite
into a white handkerchief?

The notion's absurd. Yet despite these
head-gears and thinking caps
appointing nature to our will, we suffer

as he of the wild medicines suffered.
Who still put the mistletoe up, old
'kissing bundle' among the festive lights,

and in a lull between the music
and the chat, come to countenance ourselves
as sprigs of spirit born vulnerable.

Millennium

The mill of traffic unhinges. Bleep and glare
dwindle to silence and to grey.
We take in the high broken window
through which birds loop, the chimney sprouting
a sycamore tree. Our Thomas Street's
slovenly ancient: 'pound' shops
hold; steaming Guinness stacks; all that runs
to ruin's illumined by fine art
students and Harry Clarke! While yet
a big yellow crane lifts something gone bust—
the old tailor's bereft, and won't be back.
Further, Robert Emmet is hanged,
drawn and quartered, in a heroin fix
outside St. Catherine's. But Digital Hub, how
are you? And cobble lane, greened
by down-flow—no wild cascade, just a slick
of wetness sliming some citizen's
shed, his wall and bed, since before whenever.

Harvest Woman

The high, narrow chimney-breast holds
her straw hat close to itself,
in the manner of an old, prayerful farmer.
Dust is the hat's only occupant now—

sunlight can't reach in this far.
Connotations stir. Stubble, scythed oats.
Sheaves of glossed gold, bundled
as her hair. She recalls the time

she stayed stooking after the sun had set,
her straw hat saluted by the moon.
How she smiled then: the moon
was elevating everything. How she gaped,

later, on encountering her first
lighted street-lamp. And stood under it—
charmed, full-grown, her own
transposed scarecrow, hatless and urban.

Bluebell

The factories were here even then,
the pylons fizzed above this same stretch
of sad canal. Juggernauts creamed
the asphalt hill. And sky might
be raddled with sunrise, or clouded grey,
but was traversed, either way,
with cables which I'm still in the habit
of counting, thirty years later,
from the vantage of a push-bike,
below the brow of Bluebell. Imagining
blackberry rambles, a country village
away on its own, with woods
enough to coax shade-loving flowers,
bluebells so profusely pooled
a child might pick one for a place-name
and everybody else agree to wear it
afterwards. But all I can attest to
are the pylons and factories—and this
piebald horse, standing glum,
his paddock a patch of cutaway ground.
Once, I dreamed him the original
inhabitant, old man of the place,
the king dispossessed. It was a myth
to shorten my journey. But again today
it comes around, as a startling sound
assails me up by Bluebell hill:
the trouble-boast of a rooster, flung
from a hollow heaped full of tyres
and junk metal. There, with flames
blazoned on his breast, he raises
himself, rattles his wattles in defiance

of our convoyed progress. And for
a moment I credit the earth is breaking
at my heels afresh, as a horse,
a rooster, a capercaillie—all fabulous,
indefatigable creatures restored.
And that the child has picked the bluebell.

Rocking Horse

My rocking habit comes
from the horse my father made me
as a child. Wooden, unpainted...

And now that my children
have caught me rocking to and fro
to the *Bucks of Oranmore*

played on the radio, those
uillean pipes such yelping pups,
and *Miss McCloud's Reel*

altogether uncool, I've
half a mind to tell them of that old
beloved horse, somewhere

turned to sawdust, of how
the sawdust slowly blackened
into earth, untraceable

the way the earth swallows
everything, how huge this process
and how unending, how it

will encompass us all,
such is the earth's rhythm. But
I stay shut. So it is my children,

young and well-disposed
towards the turning of world
in their direction, who suffer me

and the ancient grace notes
flitting about my head
their nods of sympathy tonight.

Journey

The cement factory complex stands
taller than this drumlin we've
begun to crest. From a mile off, the black
lettering on its forehead frowns
in our direction, its unwieldy stack
of compartments appears
through trick of the mist to lurch
across the valley towards us—
as if a juggernaut of the east, unswerving
and unstoppable, or a local
monster from a local lough, had taken
umbrage. But enlightenment as
soon breaks on our minds,
burning superstition out, clearing swamps
of their legends. And we are
certain no secret's held beyond explication
even in the well that resounds
with what seem to be human cries,
or in the thicket where a wraith
is said to shiver and levitate. Now
the saint of old, stepping onto a stone
and surfing it across the Shannon,
might look at us and be gob-smacked.
Now the serpent determined
to avenge its other half—one more
road-kill in our modern transformation
of the myth—might plunge
its head in vain against the flank
of the chariot we are embarked on. And
the ripple of apprehension passes—
a primordial reflex—just as the hulking

shape of the cement factory itself
dwindles into distance. We anticipate
air-conditioning and power showers,
plasma screens spreading out
before us impossible feats, incredible sagas,
in a hotel at the end of the motorway.

The Owl

Not that you are able to leap the fence
any more, but that you are able to imagine
leaping it. And the faces of your
long-dead parents appear to you still,
'blooming' as when they were less than half
through life. As for the owl you'll
never catch again, remember how you once
caught it, in the bog of Killoran,
to which you'd come footing turf, shortly
after your wedding. And make a play
with down-turned hands, with supple wrists
for my father before he was my father,
doing his wonder dance about you. Imagine
the owl—ghost even to itself, in a bag
swung gently home; the same owl
that in your telling flows up the chimney—
gone, with all that seemed for keeps,
into thin air, yet yours now dispassionately.

Stork

"Good pipe," the Polish plumber
says. "Good pipe", when
the elbow-bend fits into place.
These are the only words

of English he knows. And now
his boss, a farmer turned
property developer, trucks him
back from the site to where

he will drink a six-pack of beer—
in a shed, on a bale of hay.
Sleep comes; again he'll start up
to the crowing of a cock.

Yes, if still the incongruity
of cock-crow happens
to assail the world, a stone's throw
from the fast-food shack

and the smooth new motorway,
this is not a wonder to him.
He will wash and shave, for
a moment picture the white stork,

cumbersome as if caught
out of its natural element, jabbing
and flapping where it settles
to its nest in a tree at Jelenia Góra.

Dust

Then the world placed in my path
Common Earth Ball Fungus,
the thing so much a semblance
of our old football—leathery skin
flaked and tattered because left
out in all weathers—that I
simply had to kick it. The cloud
of spores unleashed a desert
about my eyes and ears and head,
and I found myself, drought's
demented preacher, prophesying
to high heaven that dust would be
continuing, dust would never
die, there was no cure but raise
dust, let dust inform, dust inspire us.

The Bear

Pigmentation on cave walls,
a man thinking
to capture an animal,
or maybe to capture an animal's
way of thinking.

And in my parish a man
who could cajole
a bull, another who'd whisper
obedience to even
the most high-spirited horse.

Neither would tell
his gift. I began to credit
the state of animal
integrity or natured separateness
could be waltzed across.

Except that this bear, he
of the delirious smile
and the murk-coloured fur,
was nobody's dancing companion.
He'd draw his own plans

up out of the ground,
where something had made
the mistake of moving,
or pluck the air down,
a sumptuous banner of smells

invisibly streaming,
and bundle it in wads about him.
What odds a berry bush
evading his juggle,
a salmon his slap, a shellfish

adrift in the sand
his lock-picking hook?
Or, if I was safe in bed, dreaming
myself a bear, this
hand become a bear's grip?

Bashō on the Dodder

Whirligig beetle,
trout, swan—the brook's
growing pains.

My face laughs
where water's skin
isn't broken.

Moss living on moss
fossils. Keepsakes of water,
water spoken for.

Give of branches.
I tap this
rag tree, poetry.

Sudden thrush
sets foot; lizard scribbles
a goodbye note.

Wind jostles
the thin poplar. Patience
leans on a stick.

I unfurl
the leaf. A prescription
of nature's.

Mess of wild
fruit, my joy
the sorrowing plum.

Heron holds still,
a beard of minnows swaying
under his chin.

He's taken to
lighting on a street-lamp—
scout of sunset, neon.

No real stand-off—
himself here, her nibs over
next the waterfall.

Juggernaut—
look. Scattered feathers,
an upset branch.

Leather-winged bat,
spinning darkness
on darkness.

Bed of sour stones,
the river's sweethearts
all in a flap.

Scrapings
and whistles—old mother's
bones, her breath.

I sleep out.
The promised wind
comes to sweep my roof.

The Badger on Orwell Bridge

might have in mind to haul between his forepaws
these parked cars, maul them into one
cacophonous, rending rejoinder to the traffic
that outside him flows. Except he's gentle.
So instead he must fall in love with the slick pelt
of the road, which he samples briefly,
dangerously, with his nose. He's come up from
an older world, past the luminous tag-art
adorning the under-bridge, come lumbering
through the tubercular slur on his name,
the last-ditch stronghold, the blood-sprayed dogs
of his baiting in a field where we stood
dumbfounded in childhood. And though
we fret for him all over again, maybe he is safer
settled here—the city's shyest customer,
unwittingly rekindling the matter of our own
animal nature. Which permits the lopsided moon
its astonished place in the pageant, swung
beyond the chimneypots and the flickering neon;
sends us following the white willows down
to dwell on the river's garnish of sensual green.

Fisherman

He seems to have set his gaze
on night descending above the Dodder wall,
against which he is leaning.

There is nothing, his whole demeanour
says, need fuss him either side,
road or river, not even the rod

which he will almost as a gesture of homage
lift, once in a while, towards
the white willow holding the far bank.

Again he'll cast, always without looking,
in token acknowledgement, perhaps,
of the breeze or a heron's

silent passing. He can't be taken
as fishing for anything. He is all disinterest.
The cigarette dangling from his lip

has some time ago gone out. When
a moth plops into the water,
its belly-flop breaking the silver skin,

he hasn't heard, he will not look.
Then a flicker of trout, a splashing hightail.
He doesn't know, being lost,

apparently, in currents of lamplight
or in his own flow. And just as not much of
anything makes you want to watch

any further, he's turned into the sudden
tugging on his hand and eye,
who now, without to do, will land the fish.

In Dodder Winter

I'm gone 7,210 wandering footsteps,
only to find myself at the river
again. It barrels in full spate
where nets of light trembled
and wavered below languid trout
last summer. I felt no ambition
then, no need of counting footsteps
or the amount of anything.

The breeze was a feather's weight,
the sun set a torque about
my neck, the river glittered. Soon,
cloud and shower, a rainbow
stood off from my shoulder.
You walked with me here. Now,
wet winter nights are only part
of the let-down between us, no trace

even of the faint red twinkle
that must have been Mars. Again
we will temper each other—I,
the poet who didn't keep his
promise; you, the painter, beginning.
While this half-submerged
washing machine spins and seethes,
spewing bubbles and suds.

Comes a chirrup from deep inside
the darkened wood, that repeats,
repeats so plaintively I must
cross the river, scramble through litter

of dead leaves, reach under
a tree's oxter. To raise as if it were
creature this mobile phone,
the querulous words of a stranger.

Hustings

It becomes a day of living where the world's
too full of air. No fault
of the thorn trees bristling at the foot
of my neighbour's garden,
though they seem to conjure the wind,
spend and still retain. More
the loud-hailing from the street—
of politicians whose cardboard promises
ride askew on lamp-posts
beyond the ambit of the trees,
sloganeering *now for the next steps, don't throw
it all away.* And such moods as
the power-seekers muster, such propulsion
of stupendous speeches,
such deeds as they would push
to fruition—chainsaws singing in the faces
of tree-folk at Coolattin, highways
grave-robbing the kings
of ancient Tara—count for less,
far less in the long reckoning than the earth's
resilience, the matter of the wind
managing, the blackbird's ode
to twilight, the teeming cast of night animals.

Continuum

She is found leaning out from the long
night's losing of her senses,
in a broken-slatted shed
the coldest turn of winter. She wears

a thin dress, otherwise only
a contusion of rainbow colours
blotches her face and knuckles and knees.
Decency does what little it can.

Sad speculation about what she
has or has not intended
stops; the TV comes on. The body
of a Victorian explorer

who died seeking a corridor through
the North West Atlantic,
is exhumed intact from the ice.
His disengaged beard, his pellucid

fingernails, make their strange appeal.
And who will see past him
to the freckled schoolgirl
hanging round the edges of things,

swinging on roped lamp-posts
after the other children
have gone home, the wispy-haired girl
who shrinks from the shouts

of the estate at nightfall, becomes
as a blur retreating where fog
rolls up from the river? Today,
the black hearse, the small white coffin.

The world the explorer sought
to widen proves, so many failures later,
too narrow to afford her
a tolerable space. While heartless hope

insists she dwells, high-spirited,
happy, in a continuum beyond
blizzard's blow and blue abominations
of neglect that still cry here through time.

Wilding

The usual things—tool-shed, flowerbed,
apple tree—are shrouded
in sodium grey. Down next the far corner,
our dog's barking at something
that won't go away. So if I
am dreaming you and you are dreaming me,
we must interrupt each other, twist
out of our thicket, tiptoe to the window
where holds a full moon, high
and red, augmenting our view.
Below, the usual animal isn't himself,
but grown fierce—and being contemplated
from the wall by a creature
at odds with what we expect: whiskered yet
too large to make domestic cat,
the long pointed ears suggesting fox,
the beaten rump a hyena's.
Ludicrous, still a rare one is there, turning
to pace the wall, back contemplating,
then—though we might linger until the last
daybreak, pleading a place for
every wilding—suddenly, irrevocably, gone.

The Road

On our desolate walk
down this particular bog road,
we see five windmills
spinning whitely in the distance
above the heathery hills.

But there's nothing we care
to say about them or
the shallow, cloud-haunted lake
away to the west of us,
and no surprises exist

any more—not the hundred
varieties of wildflower,
the thousand and one buttercups
blooming out of burnt
ground in a space the size

of our kitchen floor, not
the stone on a stone
haunched huge as any dinosaur,
not the old wrecked car
through whose bonnet

a furze bush is bursting.
For there are no endearments
we can spare, only
the dulled hurts, indifference
settling, nothing to do

but walk until the road
gives way, while all across
the blanket bog about us a swathe
of coarse grasses runs
with the will of the breeze.

Here the untenable path—
Twelve Bens jagging a far
horizon—turns us back towards
bungalow and seashore.
Despairing, at our leisure,

lost rancour, arguments
we've relinquished, the means
by which always at last
love led us to lose ourselves
only in rapture, before.

Despairing. Then skylark,
so plain a bird, ascends—
sudden, signal enough
to make us exult as up and up
he goes, disappearing

in his song, by this kindling
something fit, spirited,
sensual. So we start, each
to the other separate, together
a mystery in our mending.

The Roadside Crosses

One pierces a grassy verge
which otherwise looks innocuous,
shined with summer's gloss.

A second slants against
a wall of speckled dry-stone
swaying round the bend.

A third is sunken near the sill
of a white-washed gable
where a red geranium burns.

I count thirty seven crosses
in all—thin, sunlit,
fringed with black polythene—

thirty seven crosses troubling
the brief, lovely miles between
Cappataggle and Aughrim

with memory and warning.
A local protest. Death-sites,
approximate pinpoints

for grief not mine but pitched
along this road I take
by heart, who now might ask

if my neighbours offend
only their own elegy, or if
misfortune is all the road's fault.

Except that I am brought
back by gable sill, by speckled
stone and patch of grass,

to cognisance of the stranger
who smiled and dreamed
and was expected elsewhere,

who never once imagined
carnage would claim him here,
and in whose bloody wake

my hands must gentle
the dear, dying head, my lips
tender the contrite prayer.

Dragonfly

Don't be distracted by the blurred pastel
abdomen, the impression this
busybody gives that you are seeing multiple.
Here in sunlight she holds a draft of air
to her own will for slow seconds
on end, scans the deed that is the river,
the leaf as meal ticket. And whether
or not you play accessory, nature
commits no crime, balancing camouflage
with chance of ambush, rehearsing
the bluebottle's strung-along plea,
the bulrush that draws the dragonfly down.

Foxhall Sunset

Gaps in the whitethorns admit me to this
once and once only sunset.
Mikie, your shoes are growing weeds
in the haggard; I saw your ghost
trying to slip them on last night,
trying terribly until the moon
gave out—those shoes stood rooted.

Leena, your mottled hand
will touch your beloved chimney-breast
in vain; the only warmth
rises from the flank of an animal—
your cottage is long converted to a stable.

And maybe it's appropriate, John,
that nettles claim your proud
angry heart, for what kindness could?
But listen, I'll tell nobody,
the woman who came closest
set her love letters to you under a stone,
where they have slowly withered.

Where else did the importance go,
the immortals telling stories
while I hid by a gable, hearing and seeing
and never uttering a syllable?
Old neighbours, you should be
straightening now, shielding your eyes

against the sunbeams, with no
moral to draw from ditch or dry-stone,
no talk of tomorrow inherent
in crimson, curlew-shaped clouds,
no other day, just this darkening landscape
where your houses sit a while
and the trees of your childhood
keep their appointments with the crows.

Abbeygormican Jackdaw

The carnival bear from a field in Gurtymadden
climbs, two or three lifetimes later,
to the top of an electricity pole
in California, having remembered it

as a tree, having mistaken its drone
for the buzzing of bees. And comes down
sadder as well as wiser, to face
the gathered gawkers, the flashbulb cameras

and the dubious honey-pot
of celebrity status. All of which
has nothing to do with the robin nesting
inside a router in a carpentry workshop

in Foxhall—sixteen thousand revs
per minute, while her still self
sits on her four eggs at the one tenable still spot—
unless it's a case of needs must,

for animals. But then there's the puzzle
of the Abbeygormican jackdaw
to pick over, now he's grown conversational
about this sullen, washed-out

summer, shuffling his wet-slicked wings as he
pronounces in hoarse scraps of passable
English, "Sunny day, eh?"—again
and again until only the rain keeps me sensible.

Scaldcrow

I am fennóg in the old
tongue. I fly
out of the cave of the Morrigan
at Rathcroghan,
tap-dance
about the tips
of the iron weapons,
point them
for and into the killing.

I come down
in the world. No more the hag
rumouring war, running
war, no more
the goddess designation
though landed
here still
through dint of indefatigable
instinct—another

hungry hunter
looking nature in the eye,
taking the eye
of new-born lamb or
crocked horse:
as an amulet,
you will allow, but only in how
the lustre
shines through me now.

The Moving Bog of Derrybrien

No stately progress the bog of Derrybrien
makes, after its initial tremble, rip,
sloughing off of skin; no intact parade
of sphagnum or heather goes
downhill, only black sludge and slime,

even if somehow still one thin
pine tree towards the forefront travels
upright. Men, women shake
their heads at buckled shrubs and gates,
at streamlets choked and fields

smeared with sod-slick; children sadden
slowly in their marvelling that water
sends belly up so many fish.
Exodus quickens—as if rain and snipe
and the whistling of the wind

become too much melancholy. Or is it
the windmills, pile-driven into
the height, whirling their white geometries
across our bead on everything
we had thought familiar and forever,

derange the hills? Until, fallen
under freakish mood with no explication
other than as antidote for grief,
we find ourselves ankle-deep amid the mess,
rejoicing absurdly at this reversal

of the usual infiltration of wilderness.
Pipe-work and porch-light, we hear
our throats yell, can go hang. Then we must
lapse again, follow numbly through
the great blanket crumbling unseated—

for there never can be mended the mould
where a bog-hole slept, a system
of roots was all but tutored to float, and
the steadfast sundew overthrown
by evening's tumble has lost its double grip.

Last Movements

A thing unheard of in village memory—
crows blackening the roof
of our house, multitudes of crows.
Why didn't they feast on the barley field
as they'd always only ever done?
Were they turning into omen?
Morning sun and gust, the barley
shook its bearded heads. You declared

the day a good day for scything.
A sudden rain-shower let the breeze
relent. Now the wood appealed,
and you went, pausing on your journey
to visit an old woman who was ill,
and to settle with a customer.
These were your last movements
but for the day-long wrestle with trees,

the felling and the fall. We
retraced them later. We appropriated them
desperately. Your legendary gifts
in hurley-making, mouthed
by strangers, caused us to nod and sigh.
We dreamed you alive, set your
customary place at table, told ourselves
night would send you strolling back.

But when you came, you came
not of our will nor of your own body:
you came in a handprint planted
on the dusty metal leaf of the band-saw,
in a bundle of work-clothes from
the mortuary, in a pair of thick
spectacles, a red pencil stub, a sunlit
tree. You came and you coaxed us to cry.

Bare Branches

Arms, knuckles, nibs—poised on air—
scribble invisible signatures.
A skeletal tree, a bleak aesthetic. If I stare

long enough, the tree turns familial,
ancestral even, and I am tracing there
bloodlines, maps of kin. How they

confluence in my hands! Seamstresses
dressed in pinafore, haymaking
women, ropers of water from the well,

ballad women yeasting solid ghosts
to rise us out of work and rain. Must they
so soon go? And with them, tall

baggy-trousered men—my grandsires
of proverb—who wielded axe
and wedge, worked cross-cut, delved

in revs among pine and ash with disc-saw
and ancient tractor? I'm listening
still. The hurley turns, shaped and shone;

they warn that life's a process
designed to knock my rough edges off.
And here—I hold with it a while—

is nature's word that not last summer's
leaves alone, but every summer's,
are commemorated in the bare branches.

Le Gave

About us the Pyrenees, thronged with trees.
Le Gave, by what springs and waterfalls
did we reach this level? To lean
over a rock and fathom the feeling of falling,
to raise our eyes and imagine we soar.

Grasshoppers click amid the melting snow;
butterflies sunbathe; stone breaks
into flower. We invoke the poet Russell,
who scaled these mountains, sang these caves;
we set the eagle of legend dropping

a fish on the besieged castle at Lourdes.
And it's a case of step in, be taken
at the ankles by the cold waters of Le Gave.
It's grey matter, part of the background
that isn't noticed until it starts to run—

then you recall the lizard of Lora del Rio,
which climbed to become the town
clock's confounding hand, and I the green
lizard of Ballydoogan, whose livewire
tail once broke off to write me a red scribble.

Our Little Death

If the traffic-spying helicopter
passes over, prattling
down the bedroom chimney hole,
and the city pavements
are ripped up again, it's all

chorus to the song of our loving
in the afternoon. Here
we surmount misery's cliché,
become a pleasure
in the neck, a long string of joy.

Beyond our window, sunset
burns the clouds out,
streetlights glow. A trembling
takes root in the garden,
July's leafy damsels

offer their pale underskirts,
the flowers' blood-purple throats
pulse and sigh. Comes
the diaphanous moon, deepening;
the whole world lets go.

And our net-curtain shadows
quicken, gather to themselves
shoals of interplaying possibilities.
Labyrinthine streets slide
spinning in every direction,

the huge-headed bull jerks
to a stop, droops his weeping eye.
The notion of my death
is now, burial a hundred miles
to the west, in quiet Killoran. Would

you lie with me there? You write
a poem saying no, your
spirit might cry out of cold
loneliness, you would haul your
weed-stained pelt, your shift

of clay to a treetop, sit
wincing through the raindrops
while wind-shuffled crows
tried to appease you with their 'yea,
yea, have patience, wait,

for you are body and mind away
on a man, there's bound to be
a bus along in no time
between here and the end of eternity,
to ferry you home to Dublin'.

Mars

It stays with us, a red splintering
of the blackthorns, as down
through the hills of Derrybrien
we go. Below Duniry, in full glare
of our lights, a rabbit falls
prey to a fox. There's a pool
of darkness on the road, and this
carcase slung over the fox's
shoulder is the same creature
we saw earlier, grazing the pelt
of fox as grass. Fragranced air,
jizz of leaf, earth's life-force,
belligerence in blood, contention
between creature and creature.
Until, hours later, home to a home
away from home, we witness
the yew tree, ancient and terrible,
seeking fresh root amid
concrete, even amid smokiness,
in a regenerative circle of its
dipping branches. Will it mourn
for us, who dream ourselves
the mother and father of the house,
at our withering wave a waxen
fan of notice? Made light-headed,
weary with travel, we envision
a future familiar in everything
but that new people will supplant us,
seek to interpose themselves
as we do—just as we do now—
at the exact holding point in this
constant sundering between
what is ended and what has begun.

Tuscan Afternoon

The birds of Montecatini come to hand
under a restaurant canopy,
to pinch my bread. Not facile
in their flight, but struggling up
against the air, against their own weight
and nature. And then as if
to hell with fear, they land, snatch,
are gone. Through centuries
this little theft has happened over,
no love or kinship, no hint
of sainthood implicit, no muse making
fresh, only hunger's whet—still,
today the scrape of feather and claw
tingles my fingers, shoots
along my arm. I exit to stone
pelicans elevating fountains, architecture
of eagles flanking outsize
gods and fated heroes. Is it these
keep stealing a march on
the moment, these or the dizzying
heat or the cicadas droning
through the evergreens? Now
Michelangelo's hammer-and-chisel hands
cut marble in the white hills,
Alighieri peers through his death-mask
dolefully back at Florence,
Ghiberti's bald head sits amid
the Biblical engravings on the Gates
of Paradise, while across from
the baptistery two men go gesticulating
down a laneway—Ghiberti

himself, and Brunelleschi, old
rivals found flesh again, flying at each other
as they argue over whether
this dome, that tower, all the thronging
art of Tuscany will stand or fall.

Ghosts

They pass themselves off
as the heron standing
among shadows in crepuscular
water, the flitting bat,
the owl patenting
a figment of flying saucer.

We hear them speak
in garbled languages, trills,
ululations that open
to our every guess,
floating bodiless above these
woods and conurbations.

Even at stroke of midnight
they sing or are the wind
rushing ahead of us
where twelve birch trees
huddle white-legged
beside the tumbling Dodder.

Strange, they make us think
not at all morbidly
of the dying ground
into which we soon must sleep,
our worries done, but
rather would have us marvel

at this dream that raises
the owl, the bat, the heron,
the wind and the song.
Ghosts. The reason why we
venture. The story of ourselves
living our lucky hour.

Printed in the United Kingdom
by Lightning Source UK Ltd.
128438UK00001B/130-180/P